Thank You, God, for Christmas

Published by Standard Publishing, Cincinnati, Ohio. www.standardpub.com. Copyright © 1988, 2001, 2007 Standard Publishing. All rights reserved. Happy Day logo and trade dress are trademarks of Standard Publishing. Illustrated by Kathryn Marlin. All Scripture quotations, unless otherwise indicated, are taken from the *International Children's Bible*®, copyright © 1986, 1988, 1999, 2005 by Thomas Nelson, Inc. All rights reserved. Used by permission. Reproducible: Permission is granted to reproduce these pages for ministry purposes only—not for resale.

ISBN 978-0-7847-2054-7

14 13 12 11 10 09 08 07   7 6 5 4 3 2 1

Cincinnati, Ohio

An angel named Gabriel told Mary that soon she would have a baby boy. Her little boy would be Jesus.

**Thank you, God,
for the angel Gabriel.**

Mary told her cousin Elizabeth the good news. Elizabeth was very happy.

In Bethlehem, Mary and Joseph met a kind innkeeper. He let them stay in a warm stable because all the rooms in his inn were filled.

Thank you, God, for the kind innkeeper.

While Mary and Joseph were in Bethlehem, baby Jesus was born. The animals were the first to see God's Son!

The donkeys and cows and sheep were happy to share their warm, quiet stable with Mary and Joseph. Thank you, God, for the animals in the stable.

Many angels appeared to some shepherds that night. The angels told the shepherds that Jesus had been born. Thank you, God, for the angels.

The shepherds left their sheep and ran
to the stable to see baby Jesus.
Thank you, God, for the shepherds.

When Jesus was born, one special star shone bigger and brighter than all the other stars. Thank you, God, for the Christmas star.

Some wise men followed the special star until they found Jesus. Thank you, God, for the wise men.

**Mary and Joseph loved Jesus very much.
They took good care of him.**

Thank you, God, for Mary and Joseph.

**Jesus is God's present to the world.
He grew up to be our Savior.
Thank you, God, most of all, for Jesus.**